To Be Nicole LMonte

Sleepwalkers

Nicole Lanier Montez

Plain View Press
http://plainviewpress.net

3800 N. Lamar, Suite 730-260
Austin, TX 78756

ISBN: 978-1-935514-09-1
Library of Congress Control Number: 2012933421

Cover art: With the kind permission of © Diana Ong/Superstock
Author photograph by Glamour Shots
Cover design by Pam Knight

In Loving Memory
of
Beverly V. Montez Jones

I'm learning to live without you

Contents

II 79

I

Awaken

sound of the bomb hitting my room
boom—sham-shock bomb

hold'n big guns
control'n all the power
label'n people by the hour
hide'n behind your economic and political power
destroy'n the hood—calling us fools
scared to fight nations with equal power
so you turn around declare war on men with less power
buy'n up the hood—raising rent
mass eviction notices

sound of the bomb blow'n us up
boom—boom-va-vavooooom

don't want to go to school
what ya gonna do
21st century don't know your history
can't be a happy camper
no CD,PC, cell phone, no home
sound of the people walking over you
boom—ding-a-ling-a boom

so many religions
demons mess'n with my head
don't want eternal death wanna rise again
hear funky funky sounds when the angels come to town

listen to words
listen to sounds
brand name stores in your town
tree lined sidewalks
fresh paint on cross walks

sound of the bomb hitting my room

Nicole Lanier Montez

Choices

choose a bullet
take my chance on black man bullet
nurtured, loaded ignorance
guarantee misfire
white man bullet, detail precise
design to hit bulls eye
die sons of bitches die

Sleep On It

one eye open
floor cold
sheet shield responsibility
world keep turning
life ain't moving
death express lane
change applied for a loan
government procrastinating
skipped primary
town meeting too long
what's the use
everything is everything
called out sick

Nicole Lanier Montez

Ordinary Day

mothers making arrangements for their sons autopsied by chief medical
examiner office
special education arrested development for behaviorally challenged
students
refused to place ethnicity on SAT, disproportionate race scoring
persons of color living longer—social security age increase, making it harder
to spend our dollar
passed over for promotion new generation jim crow administration
swollen belly babies
mothers grief
fathers dead
tribe kill tribe
continent plague with acquired confusion
endless ape and white girl remakes
salesperson pretend not to notice me
refuse to acknowledge situation not directly effected
wanna be
wanna not
have
have not
right wing
wrong turn
u turn
we follow
abyss
fallen fallen
gone
bob-weave
jab
upper cut
line for temporary cash assistance
fire in the hole
aggressive takeover
downsizing up to fall
down for the count
hide and seek the declaration of oppression
one stoke away from the plow

mountains to prairie
dismantle destroy
not another 400 years of ordinary days

Nicole Lanier Montez

Direction

boys should be raised by fathers
but if boys are men and men are boys
the men will lose their childhood teaching the boys
how to be men

Arrears

attend baseball basketball swimming championship
front row seat, award ceremony best students of the year
chest poked out
smiling ear to ear
saying thanks, I'm proud too

latest kicks and clothes
flying coast to coast
waist looks like electronic store

job hop
quit
terminated
work-off books
rehearse lines
sunken chest
recycle script

accompanied by madison avenue lawyer claiming unemployment again

Nicole Lanier Montez

Perfect Package

everyday search for the perfect package
created your status features income
knew how you would comfort and kiss me

naturally, you stood in front of me
too busy looking for perfection
avoided you by moving left then right

if only I could find you

Dancing

she dances in splendid color
long soft curves
round
round
body transforming filling every space
la la la   la la   la la
if you can dance on air
the lady will give you her hand

Nicole Lanier Montez

Dream

had a dream last night
world wasn't uptight
leaders and heroes were not assassinated by men with three names

ocean aqua
air pollution free
over due apologies and reparations paid in full

racist lived on their own island, eventually they found something to hate
their neighbor for

world in harmony
alarm went off…

Awakemare

awaken to a world which thrives on competition and strife
body parts medical waste untreated defecation—ocean by products

eugenics, ponzi scheme, child brides, global warming
apologies and reparations sent to collection

injustice and displace anger
leaders and heroes have wings and monuments.

Nicole Lanier Montez

Xtra Naked

now that I've got your attention lets do this
with the lights on.
use full length mirror or shadow on the wall

1. cover all identifying features
2. slowly get into position
3. find your spot
4. start peeling your epidermis off

now, imagine a world where everyone is treated equal

Solo

everyday you see me
but your heart is blind
unaware of my existence
walk on by
there has to be an easier way to die

Nicole Lanier Montez

Save My Soul Tonight

dread dusk
  —your cold thrust
dawn tired too soon
  —cycle resume
trap in this moment
  —strangled soul
  —lying naked cold ashamed

look to you for parental guidance
  —instead you guide your parental up and down my body
trusted you once
  —never again

 dreamt you dead one thousand times
  —over and over in my head
tonight, wish me dead one thousand and one

hope you hear me tonight

Fame

touch your poster every night
dreamt being you
broke records
made history
destine hall of fame
until light shined on your door
manufactured strength
      imitation
        counterfeit
          scrub
part human, part enhancement
stolen trophies glory   placement
replaced your poster with a cross
hope, that's how to end the day

Nicole Lanier Montez

Wish

toss my coins in the fountain
pray my wish would come true
they think i'm crazy wishing for some one like you

where are the four leaf clover
where is the shooting star
where is the wishing well
need your love right now

waiting so long for you to hold me tight
images of you are all i see
need you next to me

where is the magic dust
where is the leprechaun
where are the good-luck charms
what will it take to get you in my arms

long for your embrace
for now keep on wishing
maybe my luck will change

tonight start with the stars
tomorrow crystal ball
keep trying until i get what i been wishing for

Q & A

Q. Met a lady who allows the boss to touchy feely when ever he wants. She said its okay because when she is strapped for cash or up for promotion or raise, he'll return the favor.
Ladies, is it still like that?

A.

Q. Lest we forget the magic words we learned at home and enforced in kindergarten. By the time we reach grade school we use them here and there and middle school there making there way to the back of our head. High school they fade in and out.
As an undergraduate we are not concerned with little words, we want to make big money and the graduate is concerned with making discoveries and change.
Do you remember the magic words and how frequently do you use them today?

A.

Nicole Lanier Montez

Healthy Choices

lean dreams
sour palate
limp sex
zero balls
malnutrition relationship
part-time lover husband bisexual deadbeat
need not apply
full name ain't bitch chickenhead ho
pray next man stay off just friend list
scrumptious conversations
to
intellectual debates
knead thoughts into another dimension
god fearing
fixed address match id checks license plates
hearty mains
previous selection contained empty calories
heartburn supplements
next order
deep dish love

Imprint

scented candles softly burning
romantic rhyme
everlasting embrace

afraid to believe love is real
body trembles awaiting next move

gentle sunrise cast its ray on single imprint

Nicole Lanier Montez

Time Unknown

prepared to meet the beginning
embrace death like a friend

reward, punishment could not comprehend

eyes not afraid
spirit dancing over the rainbow

jealous, could not follow

assured togetherness over the rainbow
time unknown

Alternative

balloon barrage replace bullets
hugs instead of hold ups
candy coated rain drops
housing in lieu of caskets
recreation centers not prisons
golden brick road
employment erase drugs
birth control prevent host of things
      religion
     i love you
     i love you
        i
      love
      you

Nicole Lanier Montez

Two Face

god bless and hug
turn
damn and disown

Ground Control

separated by force
taught not to trust
window view of deception
life full of turbulence

subhuman
intellectually inferior
physically superior
successfully went through detector

zero visibility cloud your thinking
life liberty happiness out of reach

disengaged seat belt
body remain restrain

amendments and isms confuse radar
misinformation passed to next generation

captain navigating life off course
flight cancelled until further notice

Nicole Lanier Montez

Big Mama

big mama, mega matriarch
where buck stops
no sass, teeth suckin', eye rollin'
head off shoulder, step wrong to big mama

big mama cook from scratch
observed manners, teeth, nails, hair
discipline hers, yours and anyone else

big mama kept family together
under her wing, became something
left nest, no regrets

gentle, aggressive, beautiful, witty
traveled many miles
body stricken with life afflictions

big mama replaced with debasing,
social promotion, gateway drugs, family clique

big mama bequest
baton, courage, wisdom
who's up for the test

Happy

wear hair according to finances
drive what suites me
dress to my fashion
elated you're the last one I'll make love too
constellation family, friends, love

candy, cigarettes, chips, minor vices
drugs, no, no

moon light setting memories
sun rays of change
unchallenged roads
celebrate our differences
live free

Nicole Lanier Montez

Crossroads

hello is someone out there
request assistance
rid life's afflictions

apply in person
no age gender race restrictions

meet at crossroads
bring faith bibles anointing oil
lord of darkness conjuring
separation virus temptation

calling all mortals, free will agents
holy armor, no charge

insatiable evil rides wind
jostling life
persuading prospective souls

meet at crossroads
bring faith bibles anointing oil
holy armor, no charge

Ghetto Love

It can't happen to me
—*why worry*
don't know
    —*didn't see*
did you hear?
    —*not interested*
would you share?
—*didn't give*

how could this be, riches country and still have poverty
if blessed with a new day,
take some ghetto love
spread 'round the world

ghetto love don't cost you nothing
no false love

you watch my back and together we'll make it through

surplus dollars—build more jails
—*no haven in the hood*

money can change a lot of things, love changes everything

take some ghetto love
    —cleanse the soul

be a good thing if the playing field was leveled
    —*endless equal hues sharing the planet*
no neighborhood depreciation, tokens, quotas, power struggles

ghetto love spread it 'round
    —maybe the only thing left to save the world

Nicole Lanier Montez

Fashionably Late (in America)

specific time given, all in attendance
event commence
several hours later you walk in
all eyes on you, smiles too
thoughts unspoken

dolt

in need of attention
feel important
it's not like you got stuck in traffic
couldn't decide what to wear

pre-meditated, main event
a.k.a.
center stage

interrupt the flow
attitudes flaring but it won't show
all eyes on you, smiles too
thoughts unspoken

self-promotion

movies and theater not your favorite venue
prefer meeting and ceremonial events
wherever there are lights and people see you walk in

ask why you do it and pretend not to comprehend
all eyes on you, smiles too
thoughts unspoken

insensitive, fashionably late
which makes you so not cool

March

for those who think we have arrived

we MARCH because the plan is not to be like you
just want life liberty happiness
lynched replaced burned for equal education
children continue to score under state achievement test level
color of our skin naturally make us person of interest
freedom of speech only applies to those wearing tailor made sheets
everybody has a bomb, tired being told what to do
stripped of natural resources identity honor

MARCH for educated law-abiding citizens
who can't move into civilized neighborhood without receiving swastika
on front door

MARCH for dead souls assembled in courthouses hoping for justice

MARCH for equal criminal justice sentencing

MARCH for recognition
abducted separated humiliated mutilated
branded showcased erased

I AM A MAN
I AM A WOMAN
I AM HUMAN

white house white men white laws
non-whites limited justice

MARCH through stone fire bullets mass arrest, twenty-four seven death
threats For wages education medical housing restaurant and front door
privileges

FREEDOM
EQUALITY
LIFE

MARCH strong brothers and sisters
sleepwalkers wake up, beat the drums

What About Me

mama keep having babies
have to stay until she comes home
can't study, play or go away
mama keep having babies
watch siblings 'round the clock
extracurricular activities
summer camp
personal time
not in my world
mama keep having babies
missed another school day
try-out
childhood
here comes another one

Nicole Lanier Montez

Speechless

shut your mouth
speak, become outcast or killed

may be true but who wanna
be told
their uncouth

shut your mouth
no diplomatic presentation gonna
change way people be

best be—
silent looker
sideliner
spectator

shut your mouth
internal dialogue, passport to long
healthy non-confrontational life

keep it locked up
speak, become outcast or killed

You

shared nest
breast
you are blood
you are pain
peace
my only request
held tongue
gray hairs sprung
you are blood
you are pain
look upon your face
hear your voice
make me run run run

Nicole Lanier Montez

Compilation of Thoughts

Past

banned from education and self-awareness
stripped of land, dignity and identification
broken families, bodies, mind and hearts

Middle-Past

freedom march
boycotts
incarceration
body bags
mass funerals
(some) recognition
(zero—little) reparation

Present

occupy america
escalated sex abuse scandals
under-educated , under-employed
not suppose to last this long

Future

?

Man Oh Man

now look here
ain't by myself
two side to every story
physical attraction
nothing more
body armor…
she said, got birth control, you go natural
nine month later family court

ready to support my miracle then…
three men stood in unison
two ruled out, due to DNA
third looking at me I at him
chick don't know who sperm fertilized egg
or
when gestation occurred

man oh man

last man standing
court clerk handed judge a document…
three new men entered court

as i drove pass the club, told my feet it was alright to dance
eyes to look into soul, penis…abstinence until mind, heart
and wedding song are one

Nicole Lanier Montez

Not a poem. Just a thought I

Want to make (some) people mad…abort gangs. Discard guns, drugs and drug paraphernalia. Stay in school and out of prisons

Reason: Enough is enough.

Crisis

read all about it!

SUPERHEROS STRIKE!
poor benefit package
no hazardous pay
long hours
hiring freeze
crime is business
rich richer richest
refuse bribe, kick back, blind eye
retire utility belt and accessories
return when new office elected
every man for himself

Nicole Lanier Montez

AWOL

abandoned post
fired emergency torch
search parties deployed
two day later
search and rescue
physical evidence recovered…

Dear America,
my eyes have seen dismembered bodies
children wielding machine guns
body fluids blanket ground
corps hors d'oevre for wild life
bullets replace stars
mass burials
wish it a bad dream
decomp confirm reality
mission…plan…all a blur
someone…something…intangible
what's land worth
new orders…old war
can't think logical about illogical situation
for this I must go

Magic

hey, want a refund
bottle guaranteed New me
rub wherever needed
results four week
eyes, nose, skin, hair, body
no change
read fine print
does not work on finished products

Nicole Lanier Montez

Winter

winter, time for resolutions
mind and heart meet over
hot chocolate and short bread cookies
who will have my heart
kiss me under cherry blossom tree
run across beach
watch fallen leaves
winter, time for resolutions
mind and heart meet over
hot chocolate and short bread cookies
deciding my fate

Lessons

wise person once told me
"look out for the devil"
no horns, tail
articulate.. sophisticated… designer suit… jean… perhaps skirt
lure you into
adultery
fornication
theft
deceit
years later encountered wise person
bragged 'bout dodging him
wise person said…they were just practice

Nicole Lanier Montez

Decisions

spring cleaning
find things you haven't
used in years
discard
donate
store for next season
sat across the table
what shall I to do with you

Dreamer

grass greener on the other side
didn't think it true
average citizen
tv...radio...newspaper...external factors
alter thoughts
not thinking 'bout boarding plane with explosives
shooting bullets from tall building
things would be different if—
less attention on who's bangin' who
break-ups
latest fashion
things would be different if—
focus on life afflictions
civility
commercials and comics okay

Nicole Lanier Montez

Check

round body
perfect dimensions
smooth
ready every night
equal opportunist
ten hand night
down low
turn over
sometime—

> fast
> slow
> hot
> cold

one on one
trade off skills
fire
swish
two minutes
possession change
protect me
five...four...three...two...one
score

Schooled

today was not like any other day
good and bad touch
hugs and kisses
what does this all mean
someone said their pocket book, suzy, wee-wee were touched
room went silent
several more kids came forward
next thing room full—police, social workers
unison… *'your not in trouble. don't be scared*
we're here to talk about safety'
all this time
right was wrong
natural turned into sexual abuse, perverted practice and host of legal
words
road to recovery
from that day on
never missed a day of school

Nicole Lanier Montez

Wow

wow, that's me
standing up for myself
makin' decisions
you ain't payin' bill
don't have to kiss ass
laugh at stupid jokes
yeah, that's me
light
empowered
little lonely
waitin' on you
gush, that's me
minus defense wounds
drama
took longer than expected
that's me

Dear God

long, long ago
prayed for a love
you sent me
storm, took my trust
rain, took my life savings
hail, broke my heart
please explain
host of inconsistent weather patterns
not asking for sunshine 365 day
just a love who ain't fakin'

Nicole Lanier Montez

Bedfellows

beautiful sunny day
blade jostle flower
think you better than me
center piece, gentle scent, assorted colors
people walk over me
ass in face
what do you have to say
flower gently replied
my friend,
you are what nature intended
vibrant, resilient
best of all my companion

Mr. Moon

mr. moon, please submit your request
man comin' home
traveled 'round world
request diamond studded sky
don't want him leaving my side
mr. moon when you see my man
you'll understand
I'm beggin' you to stay
body wrapped 'round my body
love sends me into galaxy
birds singing
doors slammin'
mr. moon, overtime wasn't approved

Nicole Lanier Montez

Broken Wing

what good is a thought contained
what good is an image deflected
what good is a voice silenced
what good is love not shared

Empty

two simple words
changed world
space time silence
endless nights
counter clockwise never changed a thing
wherever you are
sincere apology

Nicole Lanier Montez

Full

big bone
full hips
bodacious booty
went down
came back again
not afraid to be
beautiful big bone
welcome me

Candied Dreams

whenever I feel lonely
no one else will do
close my eyes
instantly you appear
butterfly kisses
bubbles
treasure hunt
snow angels
smile closed every wound
wouldn't be fair
to keep you here
maybe we can meet half way

Nicole Lanier Montez

Smooth Sailing

wouldn't it be great
if we broke-up
like we met
one on one
face to face
handshake
kiss on cheek
good-bye
walk away guilt free

Movin'

called in a jam
no time for relationship
friend with benefits
gettin' to know you
not part of plan
sweet smile
crazy laugh
good sex
never excited me
like crispy dollar bills

Nicole Lanier Montez

Sunset

start off saying goodbye
at end you'll know why
altered
compromised
negotiated
counted to ten
inhale…exhale
start over again
a word
insanity
70/30…plus…minus…no common denominator
nothing left to give
beautiful
intelligent
insatiable you

Doors

doors
rectangle, wood, metal, invisible
never know
won't open self
get up
turn the knob
discover yourself

Nicole Lanier Montez

Partner

first to know
secrets…wishes…dreams
shared best and worst
never judged
day…week…month
received phone call
new friend…lover
always last to know

Derailed

started poem in winter
distracted by snowflakes, icicles
spring cleaning
set back
summer time
words replaced with sand beach sun
fall crept in
gathered food beverage blankets
winter arrived
now, that poem

Nicole Lanier Montez

No Side driver

rolling stop
looked both ways
turned into one way street
memories
peeled off
overlooked no outlet
broken u-turn
approach with caution
lost
navigationally challenged
love drove me home

Hoodwinked

blinkin' diamonds
sparkling trees
mysterious shapes
baskets   grass   tablets
younger years, didn't care
what day or animal represented
frolic food play
historians say HE was not born on that day
Good Book, no verse exist, rabbit, candy, colored eggs
body, blood of christ
not everything sells itself
side kick sometimes help
jesus, pimped again

Nicole Lanier Montez

In the Breeze

catholic baptist episcopal jehovah witness methodist muslim
non-denomination   protestant   seven day adventist,
just to name a few
dabbled
studied
church hopped
prodigal child
don't think i'll make it in
secret…not religion…relationship

Self Preservation

red white blue
united in green
infinitely uneven

Nicole Lanier Montez

Disarmed and Possibly Dangerous

just got out
thirsty
street callin'
no escape
darkness
mischievous characters
wind surfing
no piece plan money
cold
monsters devouring meek
growing on every corner
street, first underworld teachers
minimal mainstream skills
legal options slim
economic education family castration
jackass
elephant
no definitive answer
head or tail
four corner
traffic light
ten seconds till green

Sacrifice

cancelled doctor appointment
raincheck mani pedi facial
two jobs
no vacation, depleted savings
abbreviated sleep
another day to debate
non-custodial deadbeat
attempting to modify support again
submitted several fabricated addresses
feigned injury
inoculated with chicanery
infrequent visitation
selfish position
face, smile, laughter, priceless treasures of a child
love trumps game

Nicole Lanier Montez

Second Thoughts

i'll pray for you
hear it all the time
how can you pray
while slandering my name
how can you kneel
with knee in my gut
how can your thoughts reach heaven
when your constantly thinking of ways to set me up
how can you clasp hands
when there 'round my throat
how can you see the cross
when lodge in my back
you and I get together
no thank you

Standing

she a crazy angry woman
cool calm one minute
screamin' prayin' next
she ain't crazy
life is what happen…
single mother can't make ends meet
deadbeat dad elusive
bills accumulating
caseworker non-attentive
government resources reduced
homicide drug crime unemployment infestation

knock-knock, nobody there
ring-ring, won't pick up, blame caller id

unequal wages
information withheld
inadequate education
medical care out of reach
have and have less-none-never-not

standing in the belly of systematic abuse
alters existence

Man should not be disliked because of his ignorance; and man should not be respected for refusing to change.

II

Anonymous

Hello my name is... oh I wish to remain anonymous just in case my parents are reading this story. Well, I don't know where to begin, so I'll start at the beginning. I got that from a show my nanny was watching. Anyway, everyday my nanny come to our house (occasionally she spends the weekend with me), today she's taking me to school.

On the way my nanny pushes my stroller and my mommy and daddy walk beside me. At home, nanny plays with me while my parents talk on the phone or when they have business meetings.

When nanny bathes me we have fun, she gives me a bubble bath and tickles my feet and rubs until I'm squeaky-clean. My parents are in the other room and they yell to me about how good I smell.

Nanny has been with me since day one; flu, fever, chicken pox and vaccine shots.

Today, my parents are picking me up from school. I could not wait for the day to end. I ran to the door... no mommy or daddy, just nanny waiting with that familiar smile. It was raining and nanny couldn't tell the difference, so she wiped my face until it was dry.

I almost forgot to tell you, my parents have a doggie. He's always so happy. My parents feed, walk and talk to doggie. He's thought of like a human, me a fashion accessory.

G and Shorty

Looking from the bottom up its easier to see who you are, personality stinks like the gutter. Pretend to give a damn your odors tell the true story.

Came to you for assistance can't make it here alone. You told me I'm not trying hard enough. Heard all the stories and drama. Not paid enough. Over worked, sensitivity running down the drain.

Need something to keep time flowing, ease the pain. Stop me from losing my soul.

Came to you for outreach—instead you crossed your arms.

Looking from the bottom up it's easier to see who you are.
Non-bias. Non-judgment. In theory only, pre-label the practical.
Social skills decomposed.

Dilapidated buildings one side. Townhouses the other.
Mr. & Mrs. Gentrification moving in.

Schools crowded, littered streets.
People talking. Familiar situation. Content with the environment.

Barley know who I am.
Love, hope and dreams should be immeasurable. Constricted by design, manipulated by experiment. How do you measure zero?

We came to you for assistance, refused to let us in. As if we were garbage and your trash can was full.

Tiny Mystery

Tiny mystery living inside of me. If anyone knew you were here, they would try and stop me.
Not doing this to fill a void. Not in need of unconditional love.

Many will try and decide my fate. Who are they to give me advice, judging my age and sexual appetite.

What will she do now, no life of her own

It wasn't like we didn't take precautions. Won't huff and puff to get my point across. Knew love wouldn't be enough
Pampers medicine food clothes
Medicine food clothes pampers
Food clothes pampers medicine
Clothes pampers medicine food

Who are you?
What will you be?
Never know. Doctor said we were not compatible.

Someone whispered she's got her life back

Tiny mystery no more. No one asked your name
An angel came down with a smile said we'll take care of pampers,
food, medicine and clothes and your love is enough.

Gold Plated Flatware Set

Melanie and Michael married today. Everyone knew the marriage wouldn't last but they toasted to their brief happiness.
They received beautiful wedding gifts. Melanie cherished every one. Michael, only one.

Melanie led a peaceful life and after they married she begun to notice Michael enjoyed petty hustling rather than nine to five. Lived beyond his means and told grandiose lies.

Bills added up and Melanie checking account depleted.
Melanie and Michael began to fight but Michael was a good lover and sweet talker so Melanie let it go... but not for long. Michael could not satisfy Melanie on sex alone.

Melanie outgrew Michael and wanted much, much more. Melanie tried to move on. Somehow Michael convinced his wife to stay, said he would try harder but he lied. He was not the man for Melanie though he tried. Melanie thought a man should be strong and defend the house, she felt there were two pussy in the house.

Melanie divorced Michael and life changed. Michael didn't want the bills he accumulated. Just the gold plated flatware set.

Melanie's life is great. Account out of the red. No collect calls from Michael asking to bail him out.

Rumor has it Michael sweet talked ladies prior to their divorce, smooth criminal scooping unsuspecting prey. No personality of his own, he'll transform into the person that you are. Fool you into thinking you found your soul mate, he's a fake. Savvy. Upgrade lines.

Can't tell you anything else, end of story. As for the gold plated flatware set... probably tarnished.

Iron Horse

Trains all screwed up. Take the uptown to go downtown. Congestion confusion.

Its too hot to stand underground in the summer and too cold to stand above ground in the winter.

Batteries, candy and toys for sale. People, singing and dancing for money. Some had no theme, just give up the green. Change will do too.

Passenger didn't make it to the nail salon, decided upon self-manicure. Cuticles one side and nails on the other. Never occurred how unsanitary this self-manicure was.

Meanwhile, the crowd grew and everyone held their position by the door. In the center of the train, there was room for fifteen more.

School children enter; not enough seats? They didn't care, when the train pulled off and stopped they all shouted in unison Wooooooooh!

Couple things have improve
Graffiti free trains
Heat in the winter, air condition in the summer
Window seal gum free
Gum-less floor
Pregnant women and the elderly sometime stand

Just when you think everything is going smooth, the conductor makes an announcement—

DUE TO CONSTRUCTION, THIS TRAIN IS GOING OUT OF SERVICE. TAKE THE NEXT TRAIN ENTERING THE STATION AND HAVE A NICE DAY!

This Business Is Not Mine

Don't expect you to be on this earth very long. You disagree with the rules but you know how to play the game.
Always respond in kind toward others when they deserve to be spit on.

Confess sometime you forget to thank God for all your blessings but that won't be the reason for your early departure.

You see, people come and go. Beautiful people leave faster than others; While abusers, murderers, liars, thieves and many, many more continue to walk the earth.
Ask the question. The reply, this business in not mine.

You continue to be genuinely respectful and humble. Others alter their schedule to and from work and never park in the same space.
Check caller ID. Turn on TV, breaking news…another kidnapping. Homicide. War.

Ask why they continue to walk the earth or remain in powerful positions?
Why do you allow them to multiply?
Again, this business is not mine.

Ms. Cherry, PTA President. Made dinners for the homeless, organized fundraisers for the less fortunate, died at thirty-four.

Aunt June died before her time. Should have been Uncle Frosty, treat family like unwelcome guest. Never see him at family events.

G and Shorty, fatally wounded by stray bullets.
Sudden Infant Death Syndrome; cause of death for baby Love.

Beautiful people are always placed on short detail. They work hard. Make a difference in someone life. Give freely and expect nothing in return. Never brag about their accomplishments and seldom complain.

Come to the conclusion, this business is not mine.

Proof

Sales associate left center right
Will not take their eyes off me.
Pretending to give me space.
Made a legal purchase; merchandise still disappearing.

Watching me, who watching you?
No spare eyes watching never in doubt but if everybody watching me.
How is merchandise walking out?

No spare eyes watching never in doubt.

Stopped at the same traffic light, pulled me over and you have the out-of-state plates. Temporarily detained, your half way home with your score.

No spare eyes watching never in doubt

Eyes wide shut. Walked passed lady liberty, should have been detained.
Welcome to America. Treated better than blood that built her.
Watching me, who watching you.
No spare eyes watching never in doubt.

Nightwalker

When the sun goes down, lose my identity.
Moon light creeping in telling me it's time to begin.
Take a last look and then transform; Brunette, red-head, blonde.
Lipstick. Tits. Pussy. Ass, natural ingredients to make a man hard.

Monday through Thursday walk the street.
Friday through Saturday private clients.
Sunday take a break.

When the sun goes down, lose my identity. Moons light creeping in telling
me it's time to begin.
The best at what I do.
S&M
Fantasy
Just turning eighteen, never been blown. Never deny a man's desire. Equal
opportunist giver-taker.

When he looks into my eyes, he won't remember color, all he wants is the
deep juicy thing. One told me I was his guardian angel. Spread my wings
and let him come inside. In the morning when he wakes its back to that
aggressive deceptive and cunning place, just some of the ingredients of the
working class world.
Another said I was his private dancer. Dancing to any beat or we make our
own. The message in your movement tells me you'll be back for more.

Object of your desire. Flesh and fantasy; masquerade goes on.

Take away your sorrow and loneliness. Bring pain and pleasure.

Psychologist, nurse, teacher, pediatrician, other woman, antidote. Honorary
PHD. In the corporate world this would bring additional credit but the
corporate world is inside of me, satisfying customers is what I do.

Tonight, private clients, not much of a difference.

When the sun goes down lose my identity. Moons light creeping in telling me it's time to begin. Take a last look then transform, brunette, red-head, blonde.
Lipstick, tits, pussy and ass always make a man hard.

Been this way for a long, long time, supply, demand and dead presidents.

Twisted Sister

Up in the morning forget the bathroom, pick up the phone urinating on family, friends and few associates.
Sun hasn't risen on fourth phone call; whispering, laughing, trash talking.

Pretend everything is cool. Turn your back and you change your tune.
Smiling and asking how everything is, use info against you.

Poor. Middle-class. Rich.
Saint sinner
Different hues same attitude. Got nerve calling somebody rude

spinster
unhappy
disgruntle
dejected
wanna be.
what can it be?

Sister-friend twisted too.
No significant interaction, just chitter-chatter.
Sitting there listening, smiling and shaken your head. Getting wet off the info, what's up with you?

Any age, country
low-income to mansion
Who gave you authority to talk about somebody?

Ain't sister hating, just clearing the air. What kind of sister would I be if I listened to that stupidity?
Stirring up rumors and controversy.

smart mouth
busted dreams
nature nurture
what can it be?

Spreading ills like a wild witch wielding her wand
No need to fight, fire, sabotage. All you need is a taste of love
but if you don't get it soon, somebody going to kick that behind.

Nicole Lanier Montez

Not at poem. Just a thought II

watched myself walk by
radiant reflection
aged right places
smooth transition

acceptance

hundreds of ideas
age, where creativity blossoms
forty, not the new twenty
fifty, not the thirty
age is as age has been
unforgiving
endless
stunning

No Response

In my neighborhood the people walk up and down, take a look around there going here and there. No time to talk, no time to spare.

In my neighborhood players rule—
Yo, bitches over there are packing. Give me some of that honey bun-bun. I promise to eat every crumb. Let me taste those lips, hips.
I'll let you taste my hard sweet stick.

Does any body care?
We open our mouths and close our ears—would you talk to your mother like that?

Back in the day, when parents were away, children supervise by neighbors and friends. The switch is what they got if the child spoke out of place. Buck-buck was the game!
Today, gangs, guns and drugs; genocide is what it's called.

It's like an echo when we speak
No time to talk, no time to speak

You look straight at me. Open my mouth to speak, turn your head. Got me wondering if my mouthwash isn't working today.

In my neighborhood police, politicians, judges rule. You see them around election time, hustling votes, shaking hands. They tell you how their going to make things right. Get your vote and out of sight.

Your money is long, education complete. House on the grass, mine in the street. Ain't got no money but know how to speak.

In my neighborhood, freedom of religion is understood, teach our children about the Lord up above then turn around and shout out racial slurs. Argue about what religion is right.
Monday thru Saturday lie, cuss, bomb and fight.
Sunday, dressed in white.

Judgment day is near.

In my neighborhood, people dying here and there.
Crime up, jobs scarce.
Take a look around, everybody wear a frown.

Say hello, you mumble back—sound like kiss-my-ass

Police sirens in the air

Everybody stop! Up against the wall!
Hey yo, we're going to school.

BANG! BANG!

No time to stop. No time to speak.
No time to stop. No time to speak
No time
No time
No time.

About the Author

Nicole Lanier Montez, born in Mt. Vernon, N.Y., is of African-American and Mexican descent and is a poet, licensed funeral director, cosmetologist and holds a forensic psychology degree. Montez's work is bold fresh, fruitful and vibrant; questioning social, economic and religious implications that define us. Montez writes abroad and from her residence in Maryland.

CPSIA information can be obtained at www.ICGtesting.com
Printed in the USA
BVOW012314070612

292097BV00003B/1/P